# FREEDOM FOR ALL

Neville Goddard



CLASSY
PUBLISHING

**FREEDOM FOR ALL**
by Neville Goddard

Published by Classy Publishing, 2023

www.classypublishing.com
info@classypublishing.com

ISBN: 978-93-5522-324-1



Typeset in Minion Pro
Cover Design by Classy Publishing

# CONTENTS

# FOREWORD

Public opinion will not long endure a theory which does not work in practice. Today, probably more than ever before, man demands proof of the truth of even his highest ideal. For ultimate satisfaction man must find a principle which is for him a way of life, a principle which he can experience as true.

I believe I have discovered just such a principle in the greatest of all sacred writings, the Bible. Drawn from my own mystical illumination, this book reveals the truth buried within the stories of the old and new testaments alike.

Briefly, the book states that consciousness is the one and only reality, that consciousness is the cause and manifestation is the effect. It draws the reader's attention to this fact constantly, that the reader may always keep first things first.

Having laid the foundation that a change of consciousness is essential to bring about any change of expression, this book explains to the reader a dozen different ways to bring about such a change of consciousness.

This is a realistic and constructive principle that works. The revelation it contains, if applied, will set you free.

# CHAPTER 1

## The Oneness of God

HEAR, O Israel: the Lord our God is one Lord

Hear, O Israel:
Hear, O man made of the very substance of God:
You and God are one and undivided!

Man, the world, and all within it are conditioned states of the unconditioned one, God. You are this one; you are God conditioned as man. All that you believe God to be, you are; but you will never know this to be true until you stop claiming it of another, and recognize this seeming other to be yourself.

God and man,
spirit and matter,
the formless and the formed,
the creator and the creation,
the cause and the effect —
your Father and you are one.

This one, in whom all conditioned states live and move and have their being, is your I AM — your unconditioned consciousness.

Unconditioned consciousness is God, the one and only reality. By unconditioned consciousness is meant a sense of awareness; a sense of knowing *that* I AM apart from knowing *who* I AM; the consciousness of being, divorced from that which I am conscious of being.

I AM aware of being man, but I need not be man to be aware of being. Before I became aware of being someone, I, unconditioned awareness, was aware of being; and this awareness does not depend upon being someone. I AM self-existent, unconditioned consciousness. I became aware of being someone, and I shall become aware of being someone other than this that I am now aware of being. But I AM eternally aware of being, whether I am unconditioned formlessness or I am conditioned form.

As the conditioned state, I (man), might forget who I am, or where I am, but I cannot forget that I AM.

This knowing that I AM, this awareness of being, is the only reality.

This unconditioned consciousness, the I AM, is that knowing reality in whom all conditioned states – conceptions of myself – begin and end, but which ever remains the unknown knowing being when all the known ceases to be.

All that I have ever believed myself to be, all that I now believe myself to be, and all that I shall ever believe myself to be, are but attempts to know myself – the unknown, undefined reality.

This unknown knowing one, or unconditioned consciousness, is my true being, the one and only reality. I AM the unconditioned reality conditioned as that which I believe myself to be. I AM the believer limited by my beliefs, the knower defined by the known.

The world is my conditioned consciousness objectified. That which I feel and believe to be true of myself is now projected in space as my world. The world – my mirrored self – ever bears witness of the state of consciousness in which I live.

There is no chance or accident responsible for the things that happen to me or the environment in which I find myself. Nor is predestined fate the author of my fortunes or misfortunes. Innocence and guilt are mere words with no meaning to the law of consciousness, except as they reflect the state of consciousness itself.

The consciousness of guilt calls forth condemnation. The consciousness of lack produces poverty.

Man everlastingly objectifies the state of consciousness in which he abides, but he has somehow or other become confused in the interpretation of the law of cause and effect.

He has forgotten that it is the inner state which is the cause of the outer manifestation.

*As within, so without.*

—"Correspondence", the second of
The Seven Principles of Hermes Trismegistus

And in his forgetfulness, he believes that an outside God has his own peculiar reason for doing things, such reasons being beyond the comprehension of mere man. Or he believes that people are suffering because of past mistakes which have been forgotten by the conscious mind. Or again, that blind chance alone plays the part of God.

One day man will realize that his own I AM-ness is the God he has been seeking throughout the ages, and that his own sense of awareness – his consciousness of being – is the one and only reality.

The most difficult thing for man to really grasp is this: That the "I AM-ness" in himself is God. It is his true being or Father state, the only state he can be sure of. The Son, his conception of himself, is an illusion. He always knows that he IS, but that which he is, is an illusion created by himself (the Father) in an attempt at self-definition.

This discovery reveals that all that I have believed God to be I AM.

*I AM the resurrection and the life"*

—John 11:25

...is a statement of fact concerning my consciousness, for my consciousness resurrects or makes visibly alive that which I am conscious of being

*I AM the door.*

—John 10:2, 10:7, 10:9

*"All that ever came before me are thieves and robbers.*

—John 10:8

...shows me that my consciousness is the one and only entrance into the world of expression; that by assuming the consciousness of being or possessing the thing which I desire to be or possess is the only way by which I can become it or possess it; that any attempt to express this desirable state in ways other than by assuming the consciousness of being or possessing it, is to be robbed of the joy of expression and possession.

*I AM the beginning and the end.*

—Revelation 1:8, 22:13

...reveals my consciousness as the cause of the birth and death of all expression.

> *I AM hath sent me.*
>
> —Exodus 3:14

...reveals my consciousness to be the Lord which sends me into the world in the image and likeness of that which I am conscious of being to live in a world composed of all that I am conscious of.

> *I AM the Lord, and there is no God beside Me.*
>
> —Isaiah 45:5

...declares my consciousness to be the one and only Lord and beside my consciousness there is no God.

> *BE still and know that I AM God.*
>
> —Psalm 46:1

...means that I should still the mind and know that consciousness is God.

> *Thou shalt not take the Name of the Lord thy God in vain.*
>
> —Exodus 20:7

> *"I AM the Lord: that is My Name.*
>
> —Isaiah 42:8

Now that you have discovered your I AM, your consciousness to be God, do not claim anything to be true of yourself that you would not claim to be true of God, for in defining yourself, you are defining God.

That which you are conscious of being is that which you have named God. God and man are one. You and your Father are one [John 10:30].

Your unconditioned consciousness, or I AM, and that which you are conscious of being, are one.

The conceiver and the conception are one. If your conception of yourself is less than that which you claim as true of God, you have robbed God [see Philippians 2:6], the Father, because you (the Son or conception) bear witness of the Father or conceiver. Do not take the magical name of God, I AM, in vain for you will not be held guiltless; you must express all that you claim yourself to be.

Name God by consciously defining yourself as your highest ideal.

# CHAPTER 2

## The Name of God

It cannot be stated too often that consciousness is the one and only reality, for this is the truth that sets man free.

This is the foundation upon which the whole structure of biblical literature rests. The stories of the Bible are all mystical revelations written in an Eastern symbolism which reveals to the intuitive the secret of creation and the formula of escape. The Bible is man's attempt to express in words the cause and manner of creation. Man discovered that his consciousness was the cause or creator of his world, so he proceeded to tell the story of creation in a series of symbolical stories known to us today as the Bible.

To understand this greatest of books, you need a little intelligence and much intuition – intelligence enough to enable you to read the book, and intuition enough to interpret and understand what you read.

You may ask why was the Bible written symbolically. Why was it not written in a clear, simple style so that all who read it might understand it? To these questions I reply that all men speak symbolically to that part of the world which differs from their own.

The language of the West is clear to us of the West, but it is symbolic to the East; and vice versa. An example of this can be found in the Easterner's instruction:

> *If thine hand offend thee, cut it off.*
>
> —Mark 9:43

He speaks of the hand, not as the hand of the body, but as any form of expression; and thereby he warns you to turn from that expression in your world which is offensive to you.

At the same time, the man of the West would unintentionally mislead the man of the East by saying: "This bank is on the rocks." For the expression "on the rocks" to the Westerner is equivalent to bankruptcy, while a rock to an Easterner is a symbol of faith and security.

> *I will like him unto a wise man which built his house upon a rock; and the rain descended, and the floods came, and the winds blew and beat upon that house; and it fell not; for it was founded upon a rock.*
>
> —Matthew 7:24,25

To really understand the message of the Bible you must bear in mind that it was written by the Eastern mind and therefore cannot be taken literally by those of the West. Biologically, there is no difference between the East and the West. Love and hate are the same; hunger and thirst are the same; ambition and desire are the same; but the technique of expression is vastly different.

The first thing you must discover if you would unlock the secret of the Bible, is the meaning of the symbolic name of the creator which is known to all as Jehovah. This word "Jehovah" is composed of the four Hebrew letters – JOD HE VAU HE. The whole secret of creation is concealed within this name.

The first letter, JOD, represents the absolute state or consciousness unconditioned; the sense of undefined awareness; that all inclusiveness out of which all creation or conditioned states of consciousness come.

In the terminology of today JOD is I AM, or unconditioned consciousness.

The second letter, HE, represents the only begotten Son, a desire, an imaginary state. It symbolizes an idea; a defined subjective state or clarified mental picture.

The third letter, VAU, symbolizes the act of unifying or joining the conceiver (JOD), the consciousness desiring to the conception (HE), the state desired, so that the conceiver and the conception become one.

Fixing a mental state, consciously defining yourself as the state desired, impressing upon yourself the fact that you are now that which you imagined or conceived as your objective, is the function of VAU. It nails or joins the consciousness desiring to the thing desired. The cementing or joining process is accomplished subjectively by feeling the reality of that which is not yet objectified.

The fourth letter, HE, represents the objectifying of this subjective agreement. The JOD HE VAU makes man or the manifested world (HE), in the image and likeness of itself, the subjective conscious state. So the function of the final HE is to objectively bear witness to the subjective state JOD HE VAU.

Conditioned consciousness continually objectifies itself on the screen of space.

The world is the image and likeness of the subjective conscious state which created it.

The visible world of itself can do nothing; it only bears record of is creator, the subjective state. It is the visible Son (HE) bearing witness of the invisible Father, Son and Mother – JOD HE VAU – a Holy Trinity which can only be seen when made visible as man or manifestation.

Your unconditioned consciousness (JOD) is your I AM which visualizes or imagines a desirable state (HE), and then becomes conscious of being that state imagined by feeling and believing itself to be the imagined state. The conscious union between you who desire and that which you desire to be, is made possible through the VAU, or your capacity to feel and believe.

Believing is simply living in the feeling of actually being the state imagined – by assuming the consciousness of being the state desired. The subjective state symbolized as JOD HE VAU then objectifies itself as HE, thereby completing the mystery of the creator's name and nature, JOD HE VAU HE (Jehovah).

JOD is to be aware; HE is to be aware of something; VAU is to be aware as, or to be aware of being that which you were only aware of. The second HE is your visible objectified world which is made in the image and likeness of the JOD HE VAU, or that which you are aware of being.

> *And God said, Let Us make man in Our image, after Our likeness.*
>
> —Genesis 1:26

Let us, JOD HE VAU make the objective manifestation (HE) in our image, the image of the subjective state.

The world is the objectified likeness of the subjective conscious state in which consciousness abides.

This understanding that consciousness is the one and only reality is the foundation of the Bible.

The stories of the Bible are attempts to reveal in symbolic language the secret of creation as well as to show man the one formula to escape from all of his own creations.

This is the true meaning of the name of Jehovah, the name by which all things are made and without which there is nothing made that is made [John 1:3].

First, you are aware; then you become aware of something; then you become aware as that which you were aware of; then you behold objectively that which you are aware of being.

# CHAPTER 3

## The Law of Creation

Let us take one of the stories of the Bible and see how the prophets and writers of old revealed the story of creation by this strange Eastern symbolism.

We all know the story of Noah and the Ark; that Noah was chosen to create a new world after the world was destroyed by the flood.

The Bible tells us that Noah had three sons, Shem, Ham and Japheth [Genesis 6:10].

The first son is called Shem, which means name. Ham, the second son, means warm, alive. The third son is called Japheth, which means extension. You will observe that Noah and his three sons Shem, Ham and Japheth contain the same formula of creation as does the divine name of JOD HE VAU HE.

Noah, the Father, the conceiver, the builder of a new world is equivalent to the JOD, or unconditioned consciousness, I AM. Shem is your desire; that which you are conscious of; that which you name and define as your objective, and is equivalent to the second letter in the divine name (HE). Ham is the warm, live state of feeling, which joins or binds together consciousness desiring and the thing desired, and is therefore equivalent to the third letter in the divine name, the VAU. The last son, Japheth, means extension, and is the extended or objectified state bearing witness of the subjective state and is equivalent to the last letter in the divine name, HE.

You are Noah, the knower, the creator.

The first thing you beget is an idea, an urge, a desire, the word, or your first son Shem (name).

Your second son Ham (warm, alive) is the secret of FEELING by which you are joined to your desire subjectively so that you, the consciousness desiring, become conscious of being or possessing the thing desired.

Your third son, Japheth, is the confirmation, the visible proof that you know the secret of creation.

He is the extended or objectified state bearing witness of the invisible or subjective state in which you abide.

In the story of Noah it is recorded that Ham saw the secrets of his Father [Genesis 9:22], and, because of his discovery, he was made to serve his brothers, Shem and Japheth [9:25]. Ham, or feeling, is the secret of the Father, your I AM, for it is through feeling that the consciousness desiring is joined to the thing desired.

The conscious union or mystical marriage is made possible only through feeling.

It is feeling which performs this heavenly union of Father and Son, Noah and Shem, unconditioned consciousness and conditioned consciousness.

By performing this service, feeling automatically serves Japheth, the extended or expressed state, for there can be no objectified expression unless there is first a subjective impression.

To feel the presence of the thing desired, to subjectively actualize a state by impressing upon yourself, through feeling, a definite conscious state is the secret of creation.

Your present objectified world is Japheth which was made visible by Ham. Therefore Ham serves his brothers Shem and Japheth, for without feeling which is symbolized as Ham, the idea or thing desired (Shem) could not be made visible as Japheth.

The ability to feel the unseen, the ability to actualize and make real a definite subjective state through the sense of feeling is the secret of creation, the secret by which the word or unseen desire is made visible – is made flesh [John 1:14]. "And God calleth things that be not as though they were" [Romans 4:17].

Consciousness calls things that are not seen as though they were, and it does this by first defining itself as that which it desires to express, and second by remaining within the defined state until the invisible becomes visible.

Here is the perfect working of the law according to the story of Noah. This very moment you are aware of being. This awareness of being, this knowing that you are, is Noah, the creator.

Now with Noah's identity established as your own consciousness of being, name something that you would like to possess or express; define some objective (Shem), and with your desire clearly defined, close your eyes and feel that you have it or are expressing it.

Don't question how it can be done; simply feel that you have it. Assume the attitude of mind that would be yours if you were already in possession of it so that you feel that it is done.

Feeling is the secret of creation.

Be as wise as Ham and make this discovery that you too may have the joy of serving your brothers Shem and Japheth; the joy of making the word or name flesh.

# CHAPTER 4

## The Secret of Feeling

*The secret of feeling or the calling of the invisible into visible states is beautifully told in the story of Isaac blessing his second son Jacob by the belief, based solely upon feeling, that he was blessing his first son Esau.*

—Genesis 27:1-35

It is recorded that Isaac, who was old and blind, felt that he was about to leave this world and wishing to bless his first son Esau before he died, sent Esau hunting for savory venison with the promise that upon his return from the hunt he would receive his father's blessing.

Now Jacob, who desired the birthright or right to be born through the blessing of his father, overheard his blind father's request for venison and his promise to Esau. So, as Esau went hunting for the venison, Jacob killed and dressed a kid of his father's flock.

Placing the skins upon his smooth body to give him the feel of his hairy and rough brother Esau, he brought the tastily prepared kid to his blind father Isaac. And Isaac who depended solely upon his sense of feel mistook his second son Jacob for his first son Esau, and pronounced his blessing on Jacob. Esau on his return from the hunt learned that his smooth-skinned brother Jacob had supplanted him so he appealed to his father for justice; but Isaac answered and said:

> *Thy brother came with subtlety and hath taken away thy blessing.*
>
> —Isaiah 27:35

> *"I have made him thy Lord, and all his brethren have I given to him for servants.*
>
> —Isaiah 27:37

Simple human decency should tell man that this story cannot be taken literally. There must be a message for man hidden somewhere in this treacherous and despicable act of Jacob! The hidden message, the formula of success buried in this story was intuitively revealed to the writer in this manner. Isaac, the blind father, is your consciousness; your awareness of being.

Esau, the hairy son, is your present objectified world - the rough or sensibly felt; the present moment; the present environment; your present conception of yourself; in short, the world you know by reason of your objective senses. Jacob, the smooth-skinned lad, the second son, is your desire or subjective state, an idea not yet embodied, a subjective state which is perceived and sensed but not objectively known or seen; a point in time and space removed from the present. In short, Jacob is your defined objective. The smooth-skinned Jacob — or subjective state seeking embodiment or the right of birth — when properly felt or blessed by his father (when consciously felt and fixed as real) becomes objectified; and in so doing he supplants the rough, hairy Esau — or the former objectified state. Two things cannot occupy a given place at one and the same time, and so as the invisible is made visible, the former visible state vanishes.

Your consciousness is the cause of your world. The conscious state in which you abide determines the kind of world in which you live. Your present concept of yourself is now objectified as your environment, and this state is symbolized as Esau, the hairy, of sensibly felt; the first son. That which you would like to be or possess is symbolized as your second son, Jacob, the smooth-skinned lad who is not yet seen but is subjectively senses and felt, and will, if properly touched, supplant his brother Esau, or your present world.

Always bear in mind the fact that Isaac, the father of these two sons, or states, is blind. He does not see his smooth-skinned son Jacob; he only feels him.

And through the sense of feeling he actually believes Jacob, the subjective, to be Esau, the real, the objectified.

You do not see your desire objectively; you simply sense it (feel it) subjectively.

You do not grope in space after a desirable state. Like Isaac, you sit still and send your first son hunting by removing your attention from your objective world.

Then in the absence of your first son, Esau, you invite the desirable state, your second son, Jacob, to come close so that you may feel it. "Come close, my son, that I may feel you" [27:21]. First, you are aware of it in your immediate environment; then you draw it closer and closer and closer until you sense it and feel it in your immediate presence so that it is real and natural to you.

> *If two of you shall agree on earth as touching on any point that they shall ask, it shall be done for them of My Father, Which is in heaven.*
>
> —Matthew 18:19

The two agree through the sense of feel; and the agreement is established on earth — is objectified, is made real.

The two agreeing are Isaac and Jacob — you and that which you desire. And the agreement is made solely on the sense of feeling.

Esau symbolizes your present objectified world whether it be pleasant or otherwise.

Jacob symbolizes any and every desire of your heart.

Isaac symbolizes your true self – with your eyes closed to the present world – in the act of sensing and feeling yourself to be or to possess that which you desire to be or to possess.

The secret of Isaac – the sensing, feeling state – is simply the act of mentally separating the sensibly felt (your present physical state) from the insensibly felt (that which you would like to be).

With the objective senses tightly shut Isaac made, and you can make the insensibly felt (the subjective state) seem real or sensibly known, for faith is knowledge.

Knowing the law of self-expression, the law by which the invisible is made visible, is not enough.

It must be applied; and this is the method of application.

**First:** Send your first son Esau – your present objectified world or problem – hunting. This is accomplished simply by closing your eyes and taking your attention away from the objectified limitations. As your senses are removed from your objective world, it vanishes from your consciousness or goes hunting.

**Second:** With your eyes still closed and your attention removed from the world round about you, consciously fix the natural time and place for the realization of your desire.

With your objective senses closed to your present environment you can sense and feel the reality of any point in time or space, for both are psychological and can be created at will.

It is vitally important that the natural time-space condition of Jacob, that is, the natural time and place for the realization of your desire be first fixed in your consciousness.

If Sunday is the day on which the thing desired is to be realized, then Sunday must be fixed in consciousness now.

Simply begin to feel that it is Sunday until the quietness and naturalness of Sunday is consciously established.

You have definite associations with the days, weeks, months and seasons of the year. You have said time and again, "Today feels like Sunday, or Monday, or Saturday" or "This feels like Spring, or summer, or Fall, or Winter." This should convince you that you have definite, conscious impressions that you associate with the days, weeks, and seasons of the year.

Then because of these associations you can select any desirable time, and by recalling the conscious impression associated with such time, you can make a subjective reality of that time now.

Do the same with space. If the room in which you are seated is not the room in which the thing desired would be naturally placed or realized, feel yourself seated in the room or place where it would be natural. Consciously fix this time space impression before you start the act of sensing and feeling the nearness, the reality, and the possession of the thing desired. It matters not whether the place desired be ten thousand miles away or only next door, you must fix in consciousness the fact that right where you are seated is the desired place.

You do not make a mental journey; you collapse space. Sit quietly where you are and make "there-ness" "here-ness." Close your eyes and feel that the very place where you are is the place desired. Feel and sense the reality of it until you are consciously impressed with this fact, for your knowledge of this fact is based solely on your subjective sensing.

**Third:** In the absence of Esau (the problem) and with the natural time-space established, you invite Jacob (the solution) to come and fill this space – to come and supplant his brother.

In your imagination see the thing desired. If you cannot visualize it, sense the general outline of it; contemplate it. Then mentally draw it close to you. "Come close, my son, that I may feel you."

Feel the nearness of it. Feel it to be in your immediate presence. Feel the reality and solidity of it. Feel it and see it naturally placed in the room in which you are seated. Feel the thrill of actual accomplishment and the joy of possession.

Now open your eyes. This brings you back to the objective world – the rough or sensibly felt world. Your hairy son Esau has returned from the hunt and by his very presence tells you that you have been betrayed by your smooth-skinned son Jacob – the subjective, psychologically felt.

But like Isaac, whose confidence was based upon the knowledge of this changeless law, you too will say, "I have made him thy Lord and all his brethren have I given to him for servants".

That is, even though your problems appears fixed and real, you have felt the subjective, psychological state to be real to the point of receiving the thrill of that reality. You have experienced the secret of creation for you have felt the reality of the subjective.

You have fixed a definite psychological state which in spite of all opposition or precedent will objectify itself, thereby fulfilling the name of Jacob – the supplanter.

Here are a few practical examples of this drama.

**First:** The blessing or making a thing real.

Sit in your living room and name a piece of furniture, rug or lamp that you would like to have in this particular room. Look at that area of the room where you would place it if you had it. Close your eyes and let all that now occupies that area of the room vanish. In your imagination see this area as empty space – there is absolutely nothing there. Now begin to fill this space with the desired piece of furniture. Sense and feel that you have it in this very area. Imagine you are seeing that which you desired to see. Continue in this consciousness until you feel the thrill of possession.

**Second:** The blessing or the making of a place real.

You are now seated in your apartment in New York City, contemplating the joy that would be yours if you were on an ocean liner sailing across the great Atlantic.

> *I go to prepare a place for you. And if I go and prepare a place for you, I will come again, and receive you unto myself; that where I am there ye may be also.*
>
> —John 14:2-3

Your eyes are closed; you have consciously released the New York apartment and in its place you sense and feel that you are on an ocean liner. You are seated in a deck chair; there is nothing round you but the vast Atlantic. Fix the reality of this ship and ocean so that in this state you can mentally recall the day when you were seated in your New York apartment dreaming of this day at sea. Recall the mental picture of yourself seated there in New York dreaming of this day. In your imagination see the memory picture of yourself back there in your New York apartment. If you succeed in looking back on your New York apartment without consciously returning there, then you have successfully prepared the reality of this voyage.

Remain in this conscious state feeling the reality of the ship and the ocean; feel the joy of this accomplishment – then open your eyes.

You have gone and prepared the place; you have fixed a definite psychological state and where you are in consciousness there you shall be in body also.

**Third:** The blessing or making real of a point in time.

You consciously let go of this day, month or year, as the case may be, and you imagine that it is now that day, month or year which you desire to experience. You sense and feel the reality of the desired time by impressing upon yourself the fact that it is now accomplished. As you sense the naturalness of this time, you begin to feel the thrill of having fully realized that which before you started this psychological journey in time you desired to experience at this time.

With the knowledge of your power to bless you can open the doors of any prison – the prison of illness or poverty or of a humdrum existence.

> *The Spirit of the Lord God is upon me; because the Lord hath anointed me to preach good tidings unto the meek; he hath sent me to bind up the broken hearted, to proclaim liberty to the captives, and the opening of the prison to them that are bound.*
>
> —Isaiah 61:1, Luke 4:18

# CHAPTER 5

# The Sabbath

> *Six days shall work be done, but on the seventh day their shall be to you an holy day, a Sabbath of rest to the Lord.*
>
> —Exodus 31:15, Leviticus 23:3

These six days are not twenty-four hour periods of time.

They symbolize the psychological moment a definite subjective state is fixed.

These six days of work are subjective experiences, and consequently cannot be measured by sidereal time, for the real work of fixing a definite psychological state is done in consciousness.

The time spent in consciously defining yourself as that which you desire to be is the measure of these six days.

A change of consciousness is the work done in these six creative days; a psychological adjustment, which is measured not by sidereal time but by actual (subjective) accomplishment. Just as a life in retrospect is measured not by years but by the content of those years, so too is this psychological interval measured, not by the time spent in making the adjustment, but by the accomplishment of that interval.

The true meaning of six days of work (creation) is revealed in the mystery of the VAU, which is the sixth letter in the Hebrew alphabet, and the third letter in the divine name: JOD HE VAU HE.

As previously explained in the mystery of the name of Jehovah, VAU means to nail or join.

The creator is joined to his creation through feeling; and the time that it takes you to fix a definite feeling is the true measure of these six days of creation.

Mentally separating yourself from the objective world and attaching yourself through the secret of feeling to the subjective state is the function of the sixth letter of the Hebrew alphabet, VAU, or the six days of work.

There is always an interval between the fixed impression, or subjective state, and the outward expression of that state.

The interval is called the Sabbath.

The Sabbath is the mental rest which follows the fixed psychological state. It is the result of your six days of work.

*The Sabbath was made for man.*

—Mark 2:27

This mental rest which follows a successful conscious impregnation is the period of mental pregnancy, a period which is made for the purpose of incubating the manifestation.

It was made for the manifestation; the manifestation was not made for it.

Automatically you keep the Sabbath a day of rest — a period of mental rest — if you succeed in accomplishing your six days of work.

There can be no Sabbath, no seventh day, no period of mental rest, until the six days are over — until the psychological adjustment is accomplished and the mental impression is fully made.

Man is warned that if he fails to keep the Sabbath, if he fails to enter into the rest of God, he will also fail to receive the promise; he will fail to realize his desires.

The reason for this is simple and obvious. There can be no mental rest until a conscious impression is made.

If a man fails to fully impress upon himself the fact that he now has that which heretofore he desired to possess, he will continue to desire it, and therefore he will not be mentally at rest or satisfied.

If, on the other hand, he succeeds in making this conscious adjustment so that upon emerging from the period of silence or his subjective six days of work, he knows by his feeling that he has the thing desired, then he automatically enters the Sabbath or the period of mental rest.

Pregnancy follows impregnation. Man does not continue desiring that which he has already acquired. The Sabbath can be kept as a day of rest only after man succeeds in becoming conscious of being that which before entering the silence he desired to be.

The Sabbath is the result of the six days of work.

The man who knows the true meaning of these six work days realizes that the observance of one day of the week as a day of physical quietness is not keeping the Sabbath.

The peace and the quiet of the Sabbath can be experienced only when man has succeeded in becoming conscious of being that which he desires to be. If he fails to make this conscious impression he has missed the mark. He has sinned, for to sin is to miss the mark, to fail to achieve one's objective; a state in which there is no peace of mind.

> *If I had not come and spoken unto them, they had not had sin.*
>
> —John 15:22

If man had not been presented with an ideal state toward which to aim, a state to be desired and acquired, he would have been satisfied with his lot in life and would never have known sin.

Now that man knows that his capacities are infinite, knows that by working six days or by making a psychological adjustment he can realize his desires, he will not be satisfied until he achieves his every objective.

He will, with the true knowledge of these six work days, define his objective and set about becoming conscious of being it.

When this conscious impression is made it is automatically followed by a period of mental rest, a period the mystic calls the Sabbath, an interval in which the conscious impression will be gestated and physically expressed.

The word will be made flesh. But that is not the end!

The Sabbath, or rest which will be broken by the embodiment of the idea, will sooner or later give way to another six days of work as man defines another objective and begins anew the act of defining himself as that which he desires to be.

Man has been stirred out of his sleep through the medium of desire, and can find no rest until he realizes his desire.

But before he can enter into the rest of God, or keep the Sabbath, before he can walk unafraid and at peace, he must become a good spiritual marksman and learn the secret of hitting the mark or working six days — the secret by which he lets go the objective state and adjusts himself to the subjective.

This secret was revealed in the divine name Jehovah, and again in the story of Isaac blessing his son Jacob. If man will apply the formula as it is revealed on these Bible dramas he will hit a spiritual bull's eye every time, for he will know that the mental rest or Sabbath is entered only as he succeeds in making a psychological adjustment.

The story of the crucifixion beautifully dramatizes these six days (psychological period) and the seventh day of rest.

It is recorded that it was the custom of the Jews to have someone released from prison at the feast of the Passover, and that they were given the choice of having released unto them either Barabbas the robber, or Jesus the savior. And they cried, "Release Barabbas" [John 18:40]. Whereupon Barabbas was released and Jesus was crucified.

It is further recorded that Jesus the Savior was crucified on the sixth day, entombed or buried on the seventh, and resurrected on the first day.

The savior in your case is that which would save you from that which you are not conscious of being, while Barabbas the thief is your present conception of yourself which robs you of that which you would like to be.

In defining your savior you define that which you would save you and not how you would be saved.

Your savior or desire has ways ye know not of; his ways are past finding out [Romans 11:33].

Every problem reveals its own solution. If you were imprisoned you would automatically desire to be free. Freedom, then, is the thing that would save you. It is your savior.

Having discovered your savior the next step in this great drama of the resurrection is to release Barabbas, the robber — your present concept of yourself — and to crucify your savior — or fix the consciousness of being or having that which would save you.

Barabbas represents your present problem. Your savior is that which would free you from this problem. You release Barabbas by taking your attention away from your problem, away from your sense of limitation, for it robs you of the freedom that you seek. And you crucify your savior by fixing a definite psychological state by feeling that you are free from the limitation of the past.

You deny the evidence of the senses and begin to feel subjectively the joy of being free. You feel this state of freedom to be so real that you too cry out, "I am free!" "It is finished." [John 19:30].

The fixing of this subjective state — the crucifixion - takes place on the sixth day. Before the sun sets on this day you must have completed the fixation by feeling, "It is so,""It is finished."

The subjective knowing is followed by the Sabbath or mental rest. You will be as one buried or entombed, for you will know that no matter how mountainous the barriers, how impassable the walls appear to be, your crucified and buried savior (your present subjective fixation) will resurrect himself. By keeping the Sabbath a period of mental rest, by assuming the attitude of mind that would be yours if you were already visibly expressing this freedom, you will receive the promise of the Lord. For the Word will be made flesh — the subjective fixation will embody itself.

*And God did rest the seventh day from all His works.*
—Hebrews 4:4

Your consciousness is God resting in the knowledge that, "It is well," "It is finished." And your objective senses shall confirm that it is so for the day shall reveal it.

# CHAPTER 6

## Healing

The formula for the cure of leprosy as revealed in the fourteenth chapter of Leviticus is most illuminating when viewed through the eyes of a mystic. This formula can be prescribed as the positive cure of any disease in man's world, be it physical, mental, financial, social, moral — anything.

It matters not about the nature of the disease or its duration, for the formula can be successfully applied to any and all of them.

Here is the formula as it is recorded in the book of Leviticus:

> *Then shall the priest command to take for him that is to be cleansed two birds alive and clean... and the priest shall command that one of the birds be killed.... As for the living bird, he shall take it and shall dip it in the blood of the bird that was killed; and he shall sprinkle upon him that is to be cleansed from the leprosy seven times and shall pronounce him clean and shall let the living bird loose into the open field.... And he shall be clean.*
>
> —Lev. 14:4-8

A literal application of this story would be stupid and fruitless, while on the other hand, a psychological application of the formula is wise and fruitful.

A bird is a symbol of an idea. Every man who has a problem or who desires to express something other than that which he is now expressing can be said to have two birds.

These two birds or conceptions can be defined as follows:

The first bird is your present, out-pictured conception of yourself; it is the description which you would give if you were asked to define yourself – your physical condition, your income, your obligations, your nationality, family, race, and so on. Your sincere answer to these questions would necessarily be based solely upon the evidence of your senses and not upon any wishful thinking.

This true conception of yourself (based entirely upon the evidences of your senses) defines the first bird.

The second bird is defined by the answer you wish you might give in these questions of self-definition. In short, these two birds can be defined as that which you are conscious of being and that which you desire to be.

Another definition of the two birds would be the first, your present problem regardless of its nature; and the second, the solution to that problem.

For example, if you were sick, good health would be the solution. If you were in debt, freedom from debt would be the solution. If you were hungry, food would be the solution. As you have noticed, the how, the manner of realizing the solution, is not considered. Only the problem and the solution are considered.

Every problem reveals its own solution. For sickness it is health; for poverty it is riches; for weakness it is strength; for confinement it is freedom.

These two states then, your problem and its solution, are the two birds you bring to the priest. You are the priest who now performs the drama of the curing of the man of leprosy — you and your problem. You are the priest; and with the formula for the cure of leprosy you now free yourself from your problem.

First: Take one of the birds (your problem) and kill it by extracting the blood from it. Blood is man's consciousness.

> *He hath made of one blood all nations of men to dwell on all the face of the earth.*
>
> —Acts 17:26

Your consciousness is the one and only reality which animates and makes real that which you are conscious of being. So turning your attention away from the problem is equivalent to extracting the blood from the bird. Your consciousness is the one blood which makes all states living realities. By removing your attention from any given state you have drained the lifeblood from that state. You kill or eliminate the first bird (your problem) by removing your attention from it. Into this blood (your consciousness) you dip the live bird (the solution), or that which heretofore you desired to be or possess. This you do by freeing yourself to be the desirable state now.

The dipping of the live bird into the blood of the bird that was killed is similar to the blessing of Jacob by his blind father Isaac. As you recall, blind Isaac could not see his objective world, his son Esau. You too are blind to your problem, the first bird; for you have removed your attention from it and therefore you do not see it. Your attention (blood) is now placed upon the second bird (subjective state), and you feel and sense the reality of it.

Seven times you are told to sprinkle the one to be cleansed. This means you must dwell within the new conception of yourself until you mentally enter the seventh day (the Sabbath), until the mind is stilled or fixed in the belief that you are actually expressing or possessing that which you desire to be or to possess. At the seventh sprinkle you are instructed to lose the living bird and pronounce the man clean.

As you fully impress upon yourself the fact that you are that which you desire to be, you have symbolically sprinkled yourself seven times; then you are as free as the bird that is loosed. And like the bird in flight which must in a little while return to the earth, so must your subjective impressions or claim in a little while embody itself in your world.

This story and all the other stories of the Bible are psychological plays dramatized within the consciousness of man.

You are the high priest. You are the leper. You are the birds.

Your consciousness or I AM is the high priest. You, the man with the problem, are the leper. The problem, your present concept of yourself, is the bird that is killed. The solution of the problem, what you desire to be, is the living bird that is freed.

You re-enact this great drama within yourself by turning your attention away from your problem and placing it upon that which you desire to express.

You impress upon yourself the fact that you are that which you desire to be until your mind is stilled in the belief that it is so.

Living in this fixed attitude of mind, living in the consciousness that you are now that which you formerly desired to be, is the bird in flight, unfettered by the limitations of the past and moving toward the embodiment of your desire.

# CHAPTER 7

## Desire, the Word of God

*So shall My word be that goeth forth out of My mouth; it shall not return unto Me void, but it shall accomplish that which I please, and it shall prosper in the thing whereunto I sent it.*

—Isaiah 55:11

God speaks to you through the medium of your basic desires. Your basic desires are words of promise or prophecies that contain within themselves the plan and power of expression.

By "basic desire" is meant your real objective. Secondary desires deal with the manner of realization. God, your I AM, speaks to you, the conditioned conscious state, through your basic desires. Secondary desires or ways of expression are the secrets of your I AM, the all-wise Father. Your Father, I AM, reveals the first and last: "I am the beginning and the end" [Revelation 1:8, 22:13]; but never does He reveal the middle or secret of His ways. That is, the first is revealed as the word, your basic desire. The last is its fulfillment; the word made flesh. The second or middle (the plan of unfoldment) is never revealed to man, but remains forever the Father's secret.

> *For I testify unto every man that heareth the words of the prophecy of this book, if any man shall add unto those things, God shall add unto him the plagues that are written in this book; and if any man shall take away from the words of the book of this prophecy, God shall take away his part out of the book of life.*
>
> —Rev 22:18-19

The words of prophecy spoken of in the book of Revelation are your basic desires which must not be further conditioned. Man is constantly adding to and taking from these words. Not knowing that the basic desire contains the plan and power of expression, man is always compromising and complicating his desire.

Here is an illustration of what man does to the word of prophecy, his desires.

Man desires freedom from his limitation or problem. The first thing he does after he defines his objective is to condition it upon something else.

He begins to speculate on the manner of acquiring it. Not knowing that the thing desired has a way of expression all of its own he starts planning how he is going to get it, thereby adding to the word of God.

If, on the other hand, he has no plan or conception as to the fulfillment of his desire, then he compromises his desire by modifying it. He feels that if he will be satisfied with less than his basic desire, then he might have a better chance of realizing it. In doing so he takes from the word of God.

Individuals and nations alike are constantly violating this law of their basic desire by plotting and planning the realization of their ambitions; they thereby add to the word of prophecy, or they compromise with their ideals, thus taking from the word of God.

The inevitable result is death and plagues or failure and frustration as promised for such violations.

God speaks to man only through the medium of his basic desires.

Your desires are determined by your conception of yourself. Of themselves, they are neither good or evil.

> *I know and am persuaded by the Lord Christ Jesus that there is nothing unclean of itself but to him that seeth anything to be unclean to him it is unclean.*
>
> —Romans 14:14

Your desires are the natural and automatic result of your present conception of yourself.

God, your unconditioned consciousness, is impersonal and no respecter of persons [Acts 10:34, Romans 2:11].

Your unconditioned consciousness, God, gives to your conditioned consciousness, man, through the medium of your basic desires that which your conditioned state (your present conception of yourself) believes it needs.

As long as you remain in your present conscious state, so long will you continue desiring that which you now desire.

Change your conception of yourself and you will automatically change the nature of your desires.

Desires are states of consciousness seeking embodiment. They are formed by man's consciousness and can easily be expressed by the man who has conceived them.

Desires are expressed when the man who has conceived them assumes the attitude of mind that would be his if the states desired were already expressed. Now because desires, regardless of their nature, can be so easily expressed by fixed attitudes of mind, a word of warning must be given to those who have not yet realized the oneness of life, and who do not know the fundamental truth that consciousness is God, the one and only reality.

This warning was given to man in the famous Golden Rule:

> *Do unto others that which you would have them do unto you.*
>
> —Matthew 7:21

You may desire something for yourself or you may desire for another. If your desire concerns another make sure that the thing desired is acceptable to that other. The reason for this warning is that your consciousness is God, the giver of all gifts.

Therefore, that which you feel and believe to be true of another is a gift you have given him. The gift that is not accepted returns to the giver.

Be very sure then that you would love to possess the gift yourself, for if you fix a belief within yourself as true of another and he does not accept this state as true of himself, this unaccepted gift will embody itself within your world.

Always hear and accept as true of others that which you would desire for yourself. In so doing, you are building heaven on earth.

"Do unto others as you would have them do unto you" is based upon this law.

Only accept such states as true of others that you would willingly accept as true of yourself that you may constantly create heaven on earth. Your heaven is defined by the state of consciousness in which you live, which state is made up of all that you accept as true of yourself and true of others.

Your immediate environment is defined by your own conception of yourself plus your convictions regarding others, which have not been accepted by them.

Your conception of another which is not his conception of himself is a gift returned to you.

Suggestions, like propaganda, are boomerangs unless they are accepted by those to whom they are sent.

So your world is a gift you have given to yourself.

The nature of the gift is determined by your conception of yourself plus the unaccepted gifts you offered others.

Make no mistake about this; law is no respecter of persons.

Discover the law of self-expression and live by it; then you will be free. With this understanding of the law, define your desire, know exactly what you want; make certain that it is desirable and acceptable.

The wise and disciplined man sees no barrier to the realization of his desire; he sees nothing to destroy. With a fixed attitude of mind he recognizes that the thing desired is already fully expressed, for he knows that a fixed subjective state has ways and means of expressing itself of which no man knows.

*Before they ask I have answered.*

—Approx., Isaiah 65:24

*"I have ways ye know not of.*

—Approx., Isaia 42:16

*"My ways are past finding out.*

—Romans 11:33

The undisciplined man, on the other hand, constantly sees opposition to the fulfillment of his desire. And because of the frustration, he forms desires of destruction which he firmly believes must be expressed before his basic desire can be realized. When man discovers this law of one consciousness, he will understand the great wisdom of the Golden Rule, and so he will live by it and prove to himself that the kingdom of heaven is on earth.

You will realize why you should "do unto others that which you would have them do unto you." You will know why you should live by this Golden Rule because you will discover that it is just good common sense to do so, since the rule is based upon life's changeless law and is no respecter of persons.

Consciousness is the one and only reality. The world and all within it are states of consciousness objectified.

Your world is defined by your conception of yourself PLUS YOUR CONCEPTIONS OF OTHERS which are not their conceptions of themselves.

The story of the Passover is to help you turn your back on the limitations of the present and pass over into a better and freer state.

The suggestion to "follow the man with the pitcher of water" [Mark 14:13; Luke 22:10] was given to the disciples to guide them to the last supper or the feast of the Passover. The man with the pitcher of water is the eleventh disciple, Simon of Canaan, the disciplined quality of mind which hears only dignified, noble and kindly states.

The mind that is disciplined to hear only the good feasts upon good states and so embodies the good on earth.

If you to would attend the last supper — the great feast of the Passover — then follow this man. Assume this attitude of mind symbolized as the "man with the pitcher of water" and you will live in a world that is really heaven on earth.

The feast of the Passover is the secret of changing your consciousness.

You turn your attention from your present conception of yourself and assume the consciousness of being that which you want to be, thereby passing from one state to another.

This feat is accomplished with the help of the twelve disciples, which are the twelve disciplined qualities of mind [see Your Faith is Your Fortune by the same author, chapter 18].

# CHAPTER 8

## Faith

*And Jesus said unto them, Because of your unbelief; for verily I say unto you, if ye have faith as a grain of mustard seed, ye shall say unto this mountain, remove hence to yonder place; and it shall remove; and nothing shall be impossible unto you.*

—Matthew 17:20

This faith of a grain of mustard seed has proved a stumbling block to man [1Corinthians 1:23]. He has been taught to believe that a grain of mustard seed signifies a small degree of faith. So he naturally wonders why he, a mature man, should lack this insignificant measure of faith when so small an amount assures success.

"Faith," he is told, "is the substance of things hoped for, the evidence of things not seen" [Hebrews 11:1]. And again, "Through faith… the worlds were framed by the word of God, so that things which are seen were not made of things which do appear" [Hebrews 11:3].

Invisible things were made visible. The grain of mustard seed is not the measure of a small amount of faith. On the contrary, it is the absolute in faith.

A mustard seed is conscious of being a mustard seed and a mustard seed alone. It is not aware of any other seed in the world. It is sealed in the conviction that it is a mustard seed in the same manner that the spermatozoa sealed in the womb is conscious of being man and only man.

A grain of mustard seed is truly the measure of faith necessary to accomplish your every objective; but like the mustard seed you too must lose yourself in the consciousness of being only the thing desired.

You abide within this sealed state until it bursts itself and reveals your conscious claim.

Faith is feeling or living in the consciousness of being the thing desired. Faith is the secret of creation, the VAU in the divine name JOD HE VAU HE. Faith is the Ham in the family of Noah. Faith is the sense of feeling by which Isaac blessed and made real his son Jacob. By faith, God (your consciousness) calleth things that are not seen as though they were and makes them seen.

It is faith which enables you to become conscious of being the thing desired. Again, it is faith which seals you in this conscious state until your invisible claim ripens to maturity and expresses itself, is made visible.

Faith or feeling is the secret of this appropriation. Through feeling, the consciousness desiring is joined to the thing desired.

How would you feel if you were that which you desire to be?

Wear the mood, this feeling that would be yours if you were already that which you desire to be; and in a little while you will be sealed in the belief that you are. Then without effort this invisible state will objectify itself; the invisible will be made visible.

If you had the faith of a grain of mustard seed you would this day through the magical substance of feeling seal yourself in the consciousness of being that which you desire to be.

In this mental stillness or tomblike state you would remain, confident that you need no one to roll away the stone [Matthew 28:2; Mark 16:3; Luke 24:2; John 20:1]; for all the mountains, stones and inhabitants of earth are nothing in your sight [Isaiah 40:17; Daniel 4:32]. That which you now recognize to be true of yourself (this present conscious state) will do according to its nature among all the inhabitants of earth, and none can stay its hand or say unto it, "What doest Thou?" [Daniel 4:32]. None can stop this conscious state in which you are sealed from embodying itself, nor question its right to be.

This conscious state when properly sealed by faith is a Word of God, I AM, for the man so seated is saying, "I AM so and so," and the Word of God (my fixed conscious state) is spirit and cannot return unto me void but must accomplish whereunto it is sent. God's word (your conscious state) must embody itself that you may know: "I AM the Lord… there is no God beside Me" [Isaiah 45:5]. "The Word was made flesh and dwelt among us" [John 1:14], and "He sent His word and healed him" [Psalm 107:20].

You too can send your word, God's Word, and heal a friend. Is there something that you would like to hear of a friend? Define this something that you know he would love to be or to possess. Now with your desire properly defined you have a Word of God. To send this Word on its way, to speak this Word into being, you simply do this. Sit quietly where you are and assume the mental attitude of listening; recall your friend's voice; with this familiar voice established in your consciousness, imagine that you are actually hearing his voice and that he is telling you that he is or has that which you wanted him to be or to have.

Impress upon your consciousness the fact that you actually heard him and that he told you what you wanted to hear; feel the thrill of having heard. Then drop it completely. This is the mystic's secret of sending words into expression – of making the word flesh. You form within yourself the word, the thing you want to hear; then you listen, and tell it to yourself. "Speak, Lord, for thy servant heareth" [1Samuel 3:9,10].

Your consciousness is the Lord speaking through the familiar voice of a friend and impressing on yourself that which you desire to hear. This self-impregnation, the state impressed upon yourself, the Word, has ways and means of expressing itself of which no man knows. As you succeed in making the impression, you will be unmoved by appearances, for this self-impression is sealed as a grain of mustard seed and will in due season mature to its full expression.

# CHAPTER 9

## The Annunciator

The use of a friend's voice to impregnate one's self with a desirable state is beautifully told in the story of the Immaculate Conception.

It is recorded that God sent an angel to Mary to announce the birth of his son.

> *"And the angel said unto her... thou shalt conceive in thy womb, and bring forth a son... Then said Mary unto the angel, How shall this be, seeing I know not a man? And the angel answered and said unto her, The Holy Ghost shall come upon thee, and the power of the highest shall over-shadow thee; therefore also that holy thing which shall be born of thee shall be called the son of God. For with God nothing shall be impossible.*
>
> —Luke 1:30-37

This is the story that has been told for centuries the world over; but man was not told that it was written about himself, so he has failed to receive the benefit it was intended to give him.

The story reveals the method by which the idea or Word was made flesh. God, we are told, germinated or begat an idea, a son, without the aid of another. Then He placed His germinal idea in the womb of Mary with the help of an angel who made the announcement to her and impregnated her with the idea.

No simpler method was ever recorded of consciousness impregnating itself than is found in the story of the Immaculate Conception.

The four characters in this drama of creation are the Father, the Son, Mary, and the Angel.

The Father symbolizes your consciousness. The Son symbolizes your desire. Mary symbolizes your receptive attitude of mind. And the Angel symbolizes the method used to make the impregnation.

The drama unfolds in this manner. The Father begets a Son without the aid of another.

You define your objective; you clarify your desire without the help or suggestion of another.

Then the Father selects that angel who is best qualified to bear this message or germinal possibility to Mary.

You select the person in your world who would be sincerely thrilled in witnessing the fulfillment of your desire.

Then Mary learns through the angel that she has already conceived a Son without the aid of man.

You assume a receptive attitude of mind, a listening attitude, and imagine you are hearing the voice of the one you have chosen to tell you what you desire to know. Imagine that you hear him tell you that you are and have that which you desire to be and to have. You remain in this receptive state until you feel the thrill of having heard the good and wonderful news. Then like Mary of the story, you go about your business in secret, telling no one of this wonderful and immaculate self-impregnation, confident that in due season you will express this impression.

The Father generates the seed or germinal possibility of a Son but in a eugenic impregnation. He does not convey the spermatozoa from Himself to the womb. He has it borne through another medium.

Consciousness desiring is the Father generating the seed or idea. A clarified desire is the perfectly formed seed or the only begotten Son. This seed is then carried from the Father (consciousness desiring) to the Mother (consciousness of being and having the state desired).

This change in consciousness is accomplished by the angel or imaginary voice of a friend telling you that you have already achieved your objective.

The use of an angel or friend's voice to make a conscious impression is the shortest, safest and surest way to be self-impregnated.

With your desire properly defined, you assume an attitude of listening. Imagine you are hearing the voice of a friend; then make him tell you (imagine he is telling you) how lucky and fortunate you are to have fully realized your desire.

In this receptive attitude of mind you are receiving the message of an angel; you are receiving the impression that you are and have that which you desire to be and to have. The emotional thrill of having heard that which you desire to hear is the moment of conception. It is the moment you become self-impregnated, the moment you actually feel you are now that or have that which heretofore you but desired to be or to possess.

As you emerge from this subjective experience, you, like Mary of the story, will know by your changed attitude of mind that you have conceived a Son; that you have fixed a definite subjective state and will in a little while express or objectify this state.

This book has been written to show you how to achieve your objectives. Apply the principle expressed herein and all the inhabitants of earth cannot stop you from realizing your desires.